Learning to Write
Descriptive
Paragraphs

Frances Purslow

Weigl

CALGARY
www.weigl.com

Published by Weigl Educational Publishers Limited
6325 10 Street SE
Calgary, Alberta, Canada T2H 2Z9

Website: www.weigl.com

All of the Internet URLs given in the book were valid at the time of publication. However, due to the dynamic nature of the Internet, some addresses may have changed, or sites may have ceased to exist since publication. While the author and publisher regret any inconvenience this may cause readers, no responsibility for any such changes can be accepted by either the author or the publisher.

Library and Archives Canada Cataloguing in Publication Data

Purslow, Frances
    Descriptive paragraphs / Frances Purslow.

ISBN 978-1-55388-432-3 (bound).--ISBN 978-1-55388-433-0 (pbk.)

    1. Description (Rhetoric)--Juvenile literature. 2. English language--Paragraphs--Juvenile literature. 3. Composition (Language arts)--Juvenile literature. I. Title.
PE1439.P873 2008   j808'.042   C2008-901424-3

Printed in the United States of America
1 2 3 4 5 6 7 8 9 0 12 11 10 09 08

Editor: Heather Kissock
Design: Terry Paulhus

Photograph Credits
Every reasonable effort has been made to trace ownership and to obtain permission to reprint copyright material. The publishers would be pleased to have any errors or omissions brought to their attention so that they may be corrected in subsequent printings.

Alamy: page 9T; **Corbis:** pages 8, 12T, 13B, 20; **Getty Images:** pages 3, 4, 5, 6, 9B, 10, 11, 12B, 13T, 13M, 14, 15, 19, 21, **Library of Parliament:** pages 16, 17; **Ray Joubert:** page 7.

We acknowledge the financial support of the Government of Canada through the Book Publishing Industry Development Program (BPIDP) for our publishing activities.

Table of Contents

Learning about Descriptive Paragraphs

A descriptive paragraph is a group of sentences that describes a noun. A noun is a person, a place, or a thing. A descriptive paragraph may be complete by itself, or it may be part of a longer piece of writing, such as a story.

The following is an example of a descriptive paragraph. It describes the geography of British Columbia.

British Columbia is Canada's westernmost province. It stretches from the deep, blue Pacific Ocean in the west to the towering heights of the Rocky Mountains in the east. Some of the world's most beautiful scenery lies within the vast province's borders. Endless chains of snowcapped mountains, sea-battered shorelines, rolling grasslands, ancient rain forests, and sparkling waters all help to make British Columbia's landscape the most varied in the country.

This picture shows the type of scenery that can be found in the territory of Nunavut. How would you describe what you see in this picture?

Visit **www.explorenunavut.com** to find out more about Nunavut. Make a list of the words used to describe the territory and its people on the website.

Using Words to Describe People, Places, and Things

Look at the pictures, and read the text beside each one. The text is a description of the Canadian **governor general**, the site, or the symbol shown in the picture.

Person

Michaëlle Jean is the 27th governor general of Canada. She is the first governor general of Haitian descent. Michaëlle is the youngest woman to become governor general in Canada. Before taking this important position, Michaëlle was a well-known journalist. She hosted a French news show in Canada.

Place

*In Ottawa, Canada's stately Parliament buildings attract many visitors during the year. There are three Parliament buildings in total. They are the East Block, West Block, and Centre Block. With their tall copper roofs and **Gothic** structure, these impressive buildings are a symbol of national pride.*

Thing

The national flag is one of Canada's best-known symbols. The rectangular flag has two red panels on the sides with a white panel in the centre. A red maple leaf is in the centre of the white panel. Canada's flag is twice as wide as it is long.

What words can be used to describe the people, places, and things you see in these pictures? For example, by looking at the picture of the Parliament buildings, you can tell that they are made from stone. The tall Peace Tower is the Parliament buildings' most prominent feature.

What are Adjectives?

In the description of British Columbia, you learned that the province's mountains were snowcapped and its rain forests were ancient. The words "snowcapped" and "ancient" describe two of the province's features.

To write a descriptive paragraph, you will need many describing words. Describing words are called adjectives. Adjectives describe nouns. For example, look at the following photograph of an important symbol of Canada, and read the descriptive paragraph.

The beaver is a large, furry **rodent**. It has reddish-brown fur, powerful teeth, and a large, flat tail. Beavers can swim well. They are very hard-working animals. Using small sticks, long roots, wet mud, and hard rocks, they build **dams** in forest streams. The dams create shallow ponds, where beavers build their special homes, called lodges.

The words "large" and "furry" are adjectives. They describe the noun "rodent." They tell us what a beaver looks like. Find three other adjectives in the descriptive paragraph above. Look at the image again. What other adjectives can be used to describe this animal?

Learning to Use Adjectives

Use adjectives to describe your provincial or territorial flag, or one of the provincial or territorial flags on this page.

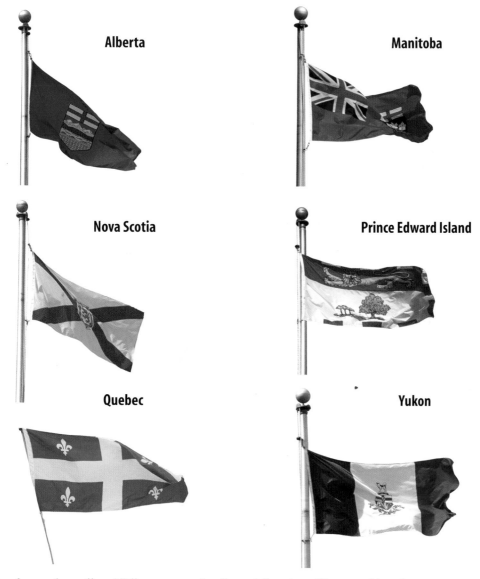

Alberta

Manitoba

Nova Scotia

Prince Edward Island

Quebec

Yukon

Words such as "red," "rectangular," and "striped" are adjectives. However, there are many other words that have a similar meaning. For example, instead of using the word "red" to describe your flag, you could use "crimson" or "scarlet." When writing the descriptive paragraph about your flag, use a thesaurus to find alternate words to describe the colours, shapes, and images.

Using the Senses

Not all descriptive paragraphs describe how something looks. Some describe how something feels to touch. Others describe how something tastes, sounds, or smells. Sometimes, a paragraph will include a description using many senses.

Read the following description of maple syrup. Note that three senses are used in the paragraph. The syrup is described as amber, sticky, and sweet. This tells you how the syrup looks, feels, and tastes.

Canada is the world's largest producer of maple syrup. Most of it comes from the province of Quebec. Maple syrup is a sticky, amber liquid. It is made from the sap of maple trees. To get the raw sap, the trees are tapped. This means a small hole is pounded into the tree trunk. The sap then runs freely into a metal bucket. The sap is clear and tasteless, but when it is boiled and the water removed by **evaporation***, it turns into a sweet, sugary syrup.*

Look at the picture of the maple syrup. Using the senses of sight, touch, and taste, think about how you would describe the syrup. You might say that the syrup is smooth and runny. What other words would you use to describe the syrup's colour, **texture**, and taste?

Using Your Senses to Describe Christmas

Read the paragraph about Christmas to learn how it was celebrated in early Canada.

On Christmas Eve, many families attended midnight masses at their local church. In Quebec, families would return home to eat a huge meal called réveillon. During the special meal, a savoury tourtière, or meat pie, was served. Other Canadians had their Christmas meal the following day. Food served often included tasty roasted goose, piping-hot potatoes, sweet cranberry sauce, and rich plum pudding. Sometimes, these festive foods were not available. On the Prairies, beaver tail and buffalo hump were roasted as part of a pioneer family's Christmas meal. The Christmas meal was a time for the family to come together and celebrate.

Today, Canadians continue to celebrate Christmas with family and friends. Many people enjoy a special meal. The meal sometimes includes corn, cranberries, and pumpkin pie. The main dish is often a big, stuffed turkey. Use adjectives to describe the taste of some of the Christmas foods in these pictures. For example, you might write "buttery corn."

Parts of a Descriptive Paragraph

A descriptive paragraph has three parts. The first part is the topic sentence. The topic sentence is usually the first sentence. It tells readers what the paragraph will be about and catches their attention. Supporting sentences generally follow the topic sentence. They provide details explaining or supporting the topic sentence.

At the end of a descriptive paragraph, a sentence wraps up, or summarizes, the ideas expressed in the paragraph. This is called the concluding sentence. It is usually a strong statement.

*Canada Day is a special time when Canadians celebrate the birth of their country. Across the large nation, communities plan exciting activities to bring Canadians together. Delicious picnics and other interesting events are a fun part of the day. Many small towns stage free concerts that feature local performers. They entertain audiences with cheery songs and lively dances. These concerts often have a **multicultural** theme. The stage comes alive with the colourful costumes and musical sounds of the cultures that make up Canada. On Canada Day, many people celebrate being Canadian.*

The topic sentence is shown in red in the paragraph about Canada Day. Can you tell which are the supporting and concluding sentences?

Identifying the Parts

Look at the photo, and write a topic sentence about a Canada Day celebration. Then, write two or three supporting sentences describing when and how the holiday is celebrated. Finally, write a strong concluding sentence.

Describing a Favourite Holiday

Read the following examples of descriptive paragraphs about Canadian holidays. Then, think about your favourite holiday. Research the origins and traditions of that holiday, and write a descriptive paragraph about it. Remember to state your main idea in a topic sentence. For example, you might write, "My favourite holiday is Easter." Then, write supporting sentences that add details about the holiday. You might describe the foods you eat and ways you decorate. Finally, end with a concluding sentence that sums up your feelings about the holiday. Be sure to include adjectives to describe nouns and use your senses to describe how nouns look, taste, smell, sound, or feel to touch.

November 11 is Remembrance Day. This is the day when Canadians honour the men and women who served in times of conflict and war. On this day, solemn events take place at war memorials across the country. **Veterans,** *soldiers, and citizens place memorial wreaths decorated with crimson poppies, colourful ribbons, and greenery on* **cenotaphs.** *Prayers and special poems are recited. Remembrance Day is a time to remember and give thanks to the brave people who have served to protect their country.*

Every year, on the second Monday of October, Canadians celebrate Thanksgiving. Thanksgiving is a harvest holiday. It represents the harvesting of the plentiful crops that skilled farmers have grown over the year. Families and friends gather to enjoy each other's company and eat a big meal. The meal includes roasted turkey, mashed potatoes, sweet cranberry sauce, and spicy pumpkin pie. Thanksgiving is a time for Canadians to be thankful for their good health, their loving families and friends, and for the fresh food on their dining tables.

Victoria Day is celebrated each year on the Monday before May 25. It honours the birth of Canada's first queen, Victoria, and symbolizes the return of the warm summer months. Many Canadians spend the Victoria Day weekend opening their summer cottages. Others head to Canada's national parks for short day hikes, family picnics, and other outdoor adventures. Throughout the day, people set off noisy firecrackers. At night, vibrant fireworks light up the sky. People look forward to Victoria Day as a time to enjoy the outdoors.

Easter is a joyful holiday that is celebrated every spring. It is an important holiday for Christians and also marks the end of winter. For many Canadian children, Easter is a time to hunt for chocolate eggs and other special treats. Early on Easter morning, young children race around their homes and backyards looking for hidden eggs and chocolate treats left by the Easter bunny. Many Canadian cities and towns host large community Easter egg hunts.

On June 24 of every year, French Canadians across the country celebrate St. Jean Baptiste Day. This day honours St. Jean Baptiste, the **patron saint** of French Canadians. It is a day for French Canadians to celebrate their rich **heritage**. Festive music concerts, colourful parades, and spectacular fireworks displays contribute to the spirit of fun this holiday holds.

Understanding Unity

All of the sentences in a descriptive paragraph should relate to the same topic. This is called unity. If a paragraph does not have unity, then one or more sentences do not relate to the main idea, as stated in the topic sentence. The following paragraph has unity. All of the sentences are about Niagara Falls.

Niagara Falls is one of Canada's best-known tourist attractions and landmarks. It is the world's greatest waterfall by **volume**. *There are 2,932 cubic metres of flowing water passing over the vast falls every second. The huge area has two main sections—the American Falls and the Horseshoe Falls. The Horseshoe Falls are located in Canada. They are about 800 metres wide and attract many visitors. About 12 million people visit Niagara Falls each year. Many take tours in a boat called* The Maid of the Mist *to experience the rumbling power of the falls. Helicopter tours also buzz above the breathtaking view.*

Which Sentence Does Not Belong?

The following paragraph does not have unity. It includes a sentence that does not relate to the main topic. Which sentence does not refer to the Grand Banks?

Europeans may have never settled in Canada if not for the Grand Banks of Newfoundland. Located in the Atlantic Ocean southeast of Newfoundland, the Grand Banks are a group of shallow, underwater **plateaus**. *They are known as prime fishing grounds for fresh cod, halibut, mackerel, and herring. Large icebergs can sometimes be seen floating in the ocean. In fact, it was this abundant supply of fish that brought European explorers and fishers to the area in the 1400s. They used the nearby land, now Newfoundland and Labrador, to process the fish they caught. From here, permanent settlements were built.*

The website **www.heritage.nf.ca/environment/ocean.html** has many facts about the Grand Banks. Use these facts to write your own descriptive paragraph about the Grand Banks. Make sure that all of the sentences have unity.

Creating Coherence

The ideas in a paragraph should flow in a logical order from beginning to end. This is called coherence. Connecting words, such as "then," "next," and "finally," help show the order of time. These connecting words are called transitions. They connect the sentences and show the sequence of events.

Other transitions can be used to describe something in order of place, such as "nearby," "above," "inside," and "at the top."

The following paragraph describes Canada's shield. Notice the transitions that provide directional cues.

Canada's official shield honours the important countries responsible for the creation of the country. In the top left corner, three lions stand as a symbol of England. To the right of the gold lions is the red lion, which represents Scotland. Below the red lion, three fleurs-de-lis are symbols for France. To their left is a golden harp that symbolizes Ireland. At the very bottom of the shield, there are three red maple leaves. They represent all Canadians. The shield is an important symbol of Canada. It honours the country's rich cultural heritage.

Put These Sentences in Order

This picture is of Canada's official mace. The following sentences describe the mace and what it is used for. Can you figure out the correct order of the sentences to create a descriptive paragraph with coherence? Look for clues to the correct order.

A. At the top of the mace sits a crown to represent the role of the British **monarchy** in Canada's past.

B. On the middle part of the mace, called the staff, there are engravings of a rose, shamrock, thistle, and maple leaf. These represent England, Ireland, Scotland, and Canada.

C. Canada's government has an official mace. It represents the power given to Canada's **House of Commons** by the king or queen to meet and decide the laws of Canada.

D. Underneath these symbols, at the foot of the staff, are engravings of more roses and thistles, as well as fleurs-de-lis. The fleurs-de-lis represent France.

E. On each side of the crown, the initials "EII" are engraved. These belong to Queen Elizabeth II.

Answers: 1. C 2. A 3. E 4. B 5. D

Tools for Paragraph Writing

What did you learn? Look at the questions in the "Skills" column. Compare them to the page number in the "Page" column. Refresh your memory about the content you learned during this part of the paragraph writing process by reading the "Content" column below.

SKILLS	CONTENT		PAGE
Using words to describe		British Columbia, Michaëlle Jean, Parliament buildings, Canadian flag	4–5
Using adjectives		beaver, provincial and territorial flags	6–7
Knowing how to write using the senses		maple syrup, Christmas	8–9
Understanding the parts of a descriptive paragraph		Canada Day	10–11
Ensuring sentences have unity		Niagara Falls, Grand Banks	14–15
Making sure the paragraph has coherence		Canada's shield, Canada's mace	16–17

Practise Writing Different Types of Sentences

Read the following paragraph about Canada's Northwest Territories. What does the author do to make the paragraph interesting?

What is it like to visit the Northwest Territories? They cover a huge amount of land, including a great deal of rugged, unpopulated wilderness. Not only is the region home to Canada's longest river—the Mackenzie River— it is also home to two of the largest lakes in the world—Great Slave Lake and Great Bear Lake. The impressive Mackenzie mountain chain runs along the western border. An endless variety of birds and wildlife live in the vast landscapes that make up the territory. It sounds so exciting! Take me there now.

Use the Internet, or visit the library to find out more information about the Northwest Territories. Then, write one or two describing sentences about what you find. Try writing one of each of the following types of sentences as well.

In a telling sentence, the writer tells about something. This sentence ends with a period.

Asking sentences ask questions. They end with a question mark.

An exclaiming sentence shows emotion. It ends with an exclamation point.

Commanding sentences give direct orders. They end with a period.

Put Your Knowledge to Use

Put your knowledge of descriptive paragraphs to use by writing about a provincial symbol.

Here is a photograph of a purple violet, the provincial flower of New Brunswick. The paragraph about the flower has a topic sentence, supporting sentences, and a concluding sentence. The sentences flow in a logical order and are related to each other. There are many adjectives throughout the text.

The province of New Brunswick chose the purple violet to be its provincial flower. This small, bluish-purple flower is a perennial. This means it grows from the same root every year and does not need to be replanted. Purple violets are stemless. Their leaves and flowers grow directly from the roots. The purple violet is mainly a spring flower, but it can bloom into early autumn. Purple violets are common in New Brunswick and can be found in the lush meadows and along the long riverbanks of the province.

Before you begin your paragraph, choose a provincial symbol. You can research the symbols at **www.canada4life.ca/ provinces.php**, or choose from the three pictures on this page. Research information about the symbol you have chosen. Then, make a list of adjectives that describe it. Include these adjectives in your descriptive paragraph.

Make sure that your paragraph has a topic sentence, supporting sentences, and a concluding sentence. Choose only sentences that relate to your topic. Finally, be sure that the ideas in your paragraph flow in a logical order from beginning to end.

Western Red Cedar - British Columbia's provincial tree

Amethyst - Ontario's provincial mineral

Ptarmigan - Nunavut's territorial bird

EXPANDED CHECKLIST

Reread your paragraph, and make sure that you have all of the following.

- ☑ My paragraph has a topic sentence.
- ☑ My paragraph has supporting sentences.
- ☑ My paragraph has a concluding sentence.
- ☑ All of the sentences in my paragraph relate to the same topic.
- ☑ All of the ideas in my paragraph flow in a logical order.
- ☑ My paragraph has adjectives.

Types of Paragraphs

Now you have learned the tools for writing descriptive paragraphs. You can use your knowledge of adjectives, the senses, parts of a paragraph, unity, and coherence to write descriptive paragraphs. There are three other types of paragraphs. You can use some of the same tools you learned in this book to write all types of paragraphs. The chart below shows other types of paragraphs and their key features.

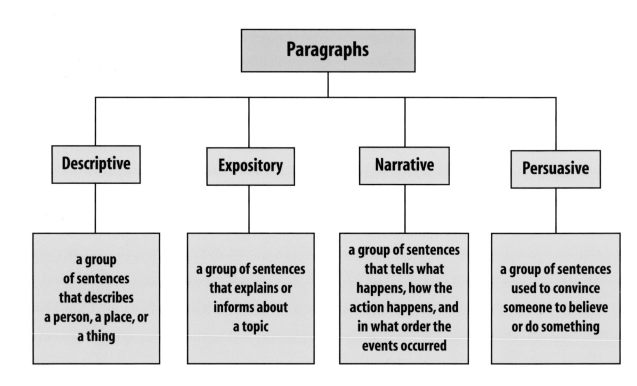

Paragraphs

Descriptive	**Expository**	**Narrative**	**Persuasive**
a group of sentences that describes a person, a place, or a thing	a group of sentences that explains or informs about a topic	a group of sentences that tells what happens, how the action happens, and in what order the events occurred	a group of sentences used to convince someone to believe or do something

Websites for Further Research

Many books and websites provide information on writing descriptive paragraphs. To learn more about writing this type of paragraph, borrow books from the library, or surf the Internet.

To find out more about writing descriptive paragraphs, type key words, such as "writing paragraphs," into the search field of your Web browser. There are many sites that teach about Canadian sites and symbols. You can use these sites to practise writing descriptive paragraphs. Begin by selecting one topic from the site. Read about the topic, and then use the checklist on page 21 to write a paragraph.

Visit *Kidzone* to learn about Canada's provincial symbols. www.kidzone.ws/geography/provinces.htm

CanadaInfo provides information about Canada's history, branches of government, and government symbols. www.craigmarlatt.com/canada

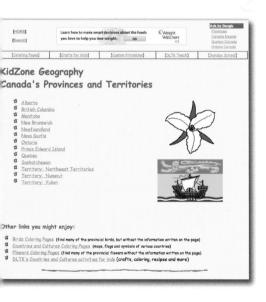

Glossary

cenotaphs: monuments to people killed in times of war

dams: walls built to hold back water

evaporation: the process of changing into a vapour or gas

Gothic: a style of building featuring pointed arches and high, steep roofs

governor general: the person who represents the British monarch in Canada

heritage: something handed down from earlier generations or the past

House of Commons: the elected representatives who meet in Ottawa to make laws

monarchy: a nation run or headed by a king or queen

multicultural: having a number of cultures existing side by side in the same country or province

patron saint: a religious person regarded as a special guardian

plateaus: large, level areas of land

rodent: a small, gnawing mammal

texture: how something feels

veterans: people who have served in the military

volume: an amount or quantity

Index